YOU KNOW YOU ARE

A GOLFER...

by Richard McChesney

illustrated by Woolly

You Know You Are A Golfer... highlights the unmistakable characteristics and passion of those among us who are wholly dedicated to the game of golf.

This is the fifth book in the "You Know You Are" book series and was compiled with the help of golfers and their families.

With 40 illustrated captions, golfers, prepare to see yourselves as others do!

Other books in the "You Know You Are" series are:

- You Know You Are A Runner...
- You Know You Are A Nurse...
- You Know You Are An Engineer...
- You Know You Are A Dog Lover...
- You Know You Are Getting Older...
- You Know You Are A Teacher...
- You Know You Are A Mother...

Visit www.YouKnowYouAreBooks.com to join our mailing list and be notified when future titles are released, or find us at www.facebook.com/YouKnowYouAreBooks, or follow us on twitter (@YouKnowYouAreBK)

YOU KNOW YOU ARE A GOLFER
WHEN YOU RISE EARLIER TO PLAY
GOLF IN THE WEEKEND THAN YOU
DO ON A WEEKDAY FOR WORK...

YOU KNOW YOU ARE A GOLFER
WHEN THE GLOVE COMPARTMENT
OVERFLOWS WITH SPARE GOLF BALLS...

YOU KNOW YOU ARE A GOLFER
WHEN YOUR WIFE HAS FORBIDDEN YOU TO
WEAR YOUR GOLFING OUTFITS IN PUBLIC...

YOU KNOW YOU ARE A GOLFER
WHEN YOU'RE ALWAYS WORKING ON YOUR SWING...

YOU KNOW YOU ARE A GOLFER
WHEN THE MOST IMPORTANT CRITERIA FOR
YOUR NEW CAR IS THE TRUNK SIZE...

YOU KNOW YOU ARE A GOLFER
WHEN YOUR FAVORITE CHANNELS ARE
'GOLF' AND 'WEATHER'...

YOU KNOW YOU ARE A GOLFER
WHEN YOU THINK PICKING UP THE WRONG
BALL IS THE EIGHTH DEADLY SIN...

YOU KNOW YOU ARE A GOLFER
WHEN THE ONLY THING YOU WISH FOR ON A DESERT ISLAND IS YOUR SAND WEDGE...

YOU KNOW YOU ARE A GOLFER
WHEN YOU START A CONVERSATION WITH
A COMPLETE STRANGER BECAUSE THEY
ARE WEARING A GOLF HAT...

YOU KNOW YOU ARE A GOLFER
WHEN THE WOODS ARE LOVELY, DARK AND DEEP...

YOU KNOW YOU ARE A GOLFER
WHEN 'PARADISE LOST' MEANS YOUR
WIFE INSISTS ON JOINING YOU FOR
YOUR REGULAR ROUND OF GOLF...

YOU KNOW YOU ARE A GOLFER
WHEN YOU CARRY YOUR GOOD LUCK BALL
WITH YOU EVERYWHERE YOU GO...

YOU KNOW YOU ARE A GOLFER
WHEN YOU LOOK FOR YOUR LOST TEES
IN THE TUMBLE DRIER...

YOU KNOW YOU ARE A GOLFER
WHEN YOUR DREAM HOUSE IS ON
THE EDGE OF A GOLF COURSE...

YOU KNOW YOU ARE A GOLFER
WHEN YOU USE YOUR HANDICAP
AS A PICKUP LINE...

YOU KNOW YOU ARE A GOLFER
WHEN YOU CHOOSE 'GOLF' OVER 'BEACH' ON A 90° SUMMER'S DAY...

YOU KNOW YOU ARE A GOLFER
WHEN YOUR GOLF SHOES ARE THE MOST
EXPENSIVE SHOES YOU OWN...

YOU KNOW YOU ARE A GOLFER
WHEN YOU DON'T CARRY A SPARE TYRE BUT YOU ALWAYS HAVE THE GOLF CLUBS...

YOU KNOW YOU ARE A GOLFER
WHEN YOU CHECK YOUR 'SET UP' IN
EVERY MIRROR YOU PASS...

YOU KNOW YOU ARE A GOLFER
WHEN YOUR WIFE STOPS WORRYING
ABOUT YOU EVER HAVING AN AFFAIR...

YOU KNOW YOU ARE A GOLFER
WHEN YOUR MOTHER-IN-LAW TAKES
UP GOLF AND YOU SUDDENLY
HAVE A NEW BEST FRIEND...

YOU KNOW YOU ARE A GOLFER

WHEN YOU ASK THE GREENKEEPER FOR
ADVICE ABOUT HOW TO TURN YOUR
BACKYARD INTO A PUTTING GREEN...

YOU KNOW YOU ARE A GOLFER
WHEN YOU USE THE WORD 'FOURSOME' IN
CONVERSATION AND THINK IT'S NORMAL...

YOU KNOW YOU ARE A GOLFER

WHEN YOU'VE BEEN KNOWN TO PRACTICE YOUR GOLF SWING WHILE TALKING TO A CO-WORKER IN THE HALLWAY...

YOU KNOW YOU ARE A GOLFER

WHEN YOUR WIFE DROPS YOU OFF AT THE LOCAL GOLF SHOP AND REFERS TO IT AS THE 'CRECHE'...

YOU KNOW YOU ARE A GOLFER
WHEN NO ROOM IS TOO SMALL FOR
YOU TO PRACTICE YOUR SWING...

YOU KNOW YOU ARE A GOLFER
WHEN YOU ADJUST YOUR GOLF CAP EVEN WHEN YOU'RE NOT WEARING ONE...

YOU KNOW YOU ARE A GOLFER
WHEN YOU CONVINCE YOUR WIFE
THAT CADDYING FOR YOU IS
SPENDING QUALITY TIME TOGETHER...

YOU KNOW YOU ARE A GOLFER
WHEN THE SIGHT OF GRASS
MAKES YOU DROOL...

YOU KNOW YOU ARE A GOLFER
WHEN YOU OWN MORE SKORTS THAN SKIRTS...

YOU KNOW YOU ARE A GOLFER
WHEN SAND LOOKS OUT OF PLACE
AT THE BEACH...

YOU KNOW YOU ARE A GOLFER
WHEN YOU GET THE URGE TO SPREAD
YOUR LEGS AND WIGGLE YOUR BOTTOM
IN A CROWDED ROOM...

YOU KNOW YOU ARE A GOLFER
WHEN AT DEATHS DOOR, HEAVEN LOOKS A
LOT LIKE YOUR FAVORITE FAIRWAY...

YOU KNOW YOU ARE A GOLFER
WHEN THE SIGHT OF A NEW GOLF
COURSE INCITES THE SAME RESPONSE
AS A HOTTIE PASSING BY...

YOU KNOW YOU ARE A GOLFER
WHEN YOU THINK THAT DRIVING TO THE
GOLF COURSE AT 4AM TO CHASE A
BALL FOR 4 HOURS IS NORMAL...

YOU KNOW YOU ARE A GOLFER
WHEN 'SNOW' IS A FOUR LETTER WORD...

YOU KNOW YOU ARE A GOLFER
WHEN YOU THINK GRASS IS MORE
PRECIOUS THAN GOLD...

YOU KNOW YOU ARE A GOLFER

WHEN YOU WOULD RATHER CONSULT 'GOLFERS DIGEST' THAN THE 'BABY NAME BOOK' FOR THE NAME OF YOUR FIRST CHILD...

So... are you a Golfer?

You have just read the fifth book in the "You Know You Are" series.

Other "You Know You Are" books are:

- You Know You Are A Runner...
- You Know You Are A Nurse...
- You Know You Are An Engineer...
- You Know You Are A Dog Lover...
- You Know You Are Getting Older...
- You Know You Are A Teacher...
- You Know You Are A Mother...

If you enjoyed this book why not join our mailing list to be notified when future titles are released – visit www.YouKnowYouAreBooks.com, or find us on facebook (www.facebook.com/YouKnowYouAreBooks), or follow us on twitter (@YouKnowYouAreBK)

Other 'You Know You Are' books include:

Visit www.YouKnowYouAreBooks.com for further details.

Printed in Great Britain
by Amazon